THAT'S A JOB?

I like ART

... what jobs are there?

by Susie Hodge

Illustrated by Elise Gaignet

Kane Miller
A DIVISION OF EDC PUBLISHING

CONTENTS

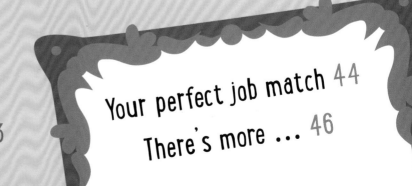

INTRODUCTION

Qualities and skills needed to work with art

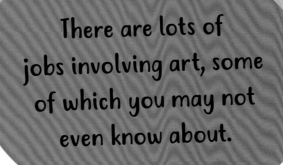

There are lots of jobs involving art, some of which you may not even know about.

Do you love art? Do you dream of working with masterpieces, or creating your own? If so, there are lots of jobs for those with an artistic flair!

From designing homes to creating video games, there are many opportunities for people who want to work with art. Each job needs people with different skills: art crime investigators need to be curious, architects need to be good at planning, and art teachers need to be great at working with people.

But there are some things that everyone who works with art should have: good attention to detail, a love for trying new ideas, and, most importantly, a passion for art.

For some of the jobs, such as game designer or art advertising director, working as part of a team is important. Others, such as children's book illustrator or artist, are best for people who like working on their own.

Whatever the job, good communication skills are often essential—you'll need to be able to make decisions and be able to express your ideas clearly. If part of your job is to create things, it's important to understand that other people will have their own thoughts and feelings—both good and bad—about your art. So being a good listener can be a really useful quality for these jobs too.

If all this sounds like you, then you're the right type of person to work with art!

This book looks at 25 different jobs that involve working with art, giving you a sneak peek into a typical day in the life of each worker. You'll learn the important stuff, like what it takes to get the job, and what duties and tasks are involved, and you'll discover the fun stuff too, such as the worst part of an auctioneer's job ...

HINT: It involves a lot of noise!

When you've read about all the different jobs in the book, turn to page 44 to find out which jobs might suit you, or page 46 to discover even more jobs!

ARTISTS

Our job is to make art! It's a dream come true. Each of us love what we do, but it takes a lot of determination—as well as talent—to be successful.

SCULPTOR

After high school, I earned a bachelor's degree in fine art, with a speciality in sculpture. I carve statues from hard materials like stone and marble. First, I create drawings of the sculpture I'm going to make. Then, I make a small model of the statue in clay—this is called a maquette. I use power tools to cut the stone into the rough shape I want. I add the smaller details with a hammer and a chisel (a tool with a blade for carving). I have to be careful— if I cut off the wrong piece, there's no going back! My job takes a lot of imagination, strength, skill, and precision.

LANDSCAPE PAINTER

I studied landscape painting when I earned my fine art degree. Now, it's my job; people pay me to create pictures of their favorite places. First, I roughly draw the landscape in a sketchbook, so that I can plot out the spacing and structure of the scene. I then copy the sketch onto paper so that it's ready to paint over. I use watercolors (paints that you add water to, in order to use). This kind of paint dries quickly, so it's great to use whether I'm working in my studio or outside. I use social media to attract new customers. That part of the job can be tiring, but I love being creative every day.

PORTRAIT ARTIST

While studying fine art in college, I found I most enjoyed creating portraits of people. I mostly work with models, but sometimes I use photographs. I use oil paints because they take a long time to dry, which means I can blend paint together on the canvas to get the colors I need. First, I use charcoal to lightly draw the person's features onto my canvas. Then, I paint. I sell portraits in my online store, and I have also had my work shown in galleries for people to buy.

CERAMICIST

I'm a ceramicist, a person who works with pottery. I trained as an apprentice with another ceramicist, then started my own business making pots and vases. I use a pottery wheel—a spinning disk I control with a foot pedal to shape the wet clay. Once the clay has been shaped into an object, it's baked in an extremely hot oven called a kiln to harden it. Then, I glaze it, which adds color and shine, to create the finished product.

SCREEN PRINTER

I learned screen printing at art school and make prints in my studio. First, I draw a design on paper and cut it out to create a block stencil. I place the stencil on top of another piece of paper or cardstock, and then put a screen, a sheet of mesh (net) stretched over a wooden frame, on top. I use a tool called a squeegee to slowly drag thick ink across the screen. The ink transfers through the screen and around the stencil, creating a print of my design. I work on many different projects at once: my own prints to sell and posters for large companies.

MURALIST

As a kid, I participated in a community mural project that sparked my passion. When I finished my fine art degree, I knew that's what I wanted to do! I'm hired by businesses to design and paint murals. I paint directly onto walls, ceilings, and huge canvases. I start off by sketching designs, based on my ideas or the ideas of the client, onto graph paper. To turn these small-scale designs into large artworks, I draw a grid onto the surface I'm painting on. I can then copy my sketches onto the surface, grid by grid. My job means a lot of work outside, in hot or cold weather!

ARTISTS: BEST AND WORST PARTS

BEST: We make a living doing what we love the most.

WORST: Art is all about opinions— not everyone will like all of our work all of the time.

ART MUSEUM CURATOR

I work in an art museum, where I plan and set up exhibitions (specialized collections of art). I have to be organized and work well with others since so many different people are needed to put on a museum exhibition. It also helps that I'm so passionate about art! I have a master's degree in art history, but I'm still always learning.

Large museums might have a team of curators who each specialize in a different kind of art, such as painting or sculpture. There's also the museum director, who is in charge of how much money the museum needs to make, and how much can be spent on art.

1

This morning, I'm planning a new exhibition based around the environment. All of the art will focus on people's impact on the planet. I suggested this theme to the museum director because it's a subject that interests a lot of people, and I think it will be popular. The museum director agreed, so my first task is to find the art.

2

I recently saw an artist's work in a gallery. He creates sculptures from recycled materials, and I think his work would be perfect for the exhibition. I call him and tell him about it, and he's interested—great! I'll head over to his studio later today to look at his work. I spend a few hours calling more artists and making appointments to visit their studios.

3

Then, I use the Internet to search for an eco-friendly sponsor for the exhibition. Sponsors often pay toward the costs of an exhibition in exchange for advertising. Having their support means we can keep museum ticket prices low. I'll present my findings to the museum director tomorrow.

MY JOB: BEST AND WORST PARTS

BEST: It's great seeing people enjoy art when an exhibition is set up and full of visitors.

WORST: Making sure all the valuable works of art arrive—and are returned—safely and on time is a lot of responsibility.

4

I finish my morning by planning how to arrange artwork in the space. I want to include some large sculptures in this exhibition, but visitors need to be able to walk around easily. I use a floor plan and a computer program to work out how many artworks to include. I decide I can have four large sculptures, and about 12 pieces of art for the walls.

5

In the afternoon, I switch my focus. Some visitors have paid for a special "curator tour." I take them through our current exhibition, giving them as much information as I can about the works of art and the artists who created them, answering questions, and sharing their enthusiasm.

6

Once the tour is over, I head out to meet the artist I spoke to this morning at his studio. He shows me a sculpture made out of plastic bottles pulled out of the ocean. I think visitors will find it fascinating. I'd love to have it in the exhibition, and the artist agrees!

7

By the time the meeting ends, it's evening, and my workday is over. But instead of heading home, I'm off to art class. Who knows ... maybe one of my paintings will be hanging in a museum one day!

9

FURNITURE MAKER

Furniture is part of our everyday lives, and it's my job to design and make beautiful and functional furniture, from tables and chairs to beds and bookcases. I studied woodworking and furniture design, then worked as an apprentice. Now, I have my own business—I sell my work to stores and private clients, as well as repairing and restoring furniture.

In school, I enjoyed shop class, where I learned to create things with wood and other materials. Making furniture requires accuracy and a lot of care. It also helps to be good at math—there's a lot of measuring to be done!

1

This morning, I'm working on a new project: a client has asked me to design some modern-style dining-room chairs. I research chairs made of different materials, including wood, plastic, and metal. Feeling inspired, I spend time sketching ideas. I decide on a chair with a cool, twisted base rather than four legs, made from a wipe-clean plastic.

2

Once I'm happy with my sketches, I spend the rest of the morning creating technical drawings of the chair, showing the size of all the parts and how they fit together. These take a long time, since everything needs to be exact: I need to carefully measure the lengths and weights of the materials. If I get a detail wrong, the parts of the chair might not fit together when I build it!

3

The morning rushes by, and I head out to buy lunch from a cafe across the street from my workshop. The cafe owner bought one of my tables, and it's great to see people using and enjoying it.

MY JOB: BEST AND WORST PARTS

BEST: It's really satisfying to make something with your hands.

WORST: Sometimes I make mistakes and have to start again.

4

After lunch, I restore a dresser that has been brought to my workshop. I sand it by hand with sandpaper to remove the dirt and stains. I spend a few hours slowly doing this—it takes care to make old furniture look good. Under the dirt, there's the beautiful original dark wood. Tomorrow, I'll apply a clear finishing oil and then it will be ready to go back to its owner.

5

Next, I return to the dining chairs. I figure out how much the materials will cost, and how long it will take me to build the chairs because I must charge the client for my time. I add it all together, and then email the estimated cost to the client with the technical drawings to see if she wants me to make the chairs. Hopefully she'll love the design and think the total price is reasonable.

6

I spend the rest of the afternoon working on a desk I'm building. It's an elaborate design, and I started the work over a month ago. It takes a lot of concentration as I cut and shape the wood with both handsaws and machine saws. I wear protective clothing and a mask, so I don't breathe in sawdust.

7

I put down my tools at 5:00 p.m., then spend the next half hour sweeping, tidying, and putting things away. I like to leave the workshop clean, with everything in its place, so I can start fresh in the morning.

8

I'm just about to head home when I get a call. It's my client— she loves the chair design and wants me to get started as soon as I can. What a great way to end the day!

ARCHITECT

My job is to design residential buildings. It combines two things I'm great at—drawing and math. It took a lot of hard work to become an architect. I earned a master's degree in architecture, got lots of experience through internships, and then studied for a state license so that I could practice. It took a long time, but it was worth it!

Along with apartment buildings and houses, architects design hospitals, schools, offices—just about any building you can think of has probably been designed by an architect!

1

For my first task of the day, another architect and I meet with a client to discuss plans for a new apartment building. I have prepared some sketches based on the client's ideas—they want the apartments to feel stylish and modern. I lay out the initial designs and talk about my ideas. I think it should have a cool white finish and a funky rooftop terrace for its residents to enjoy. The client loves it!

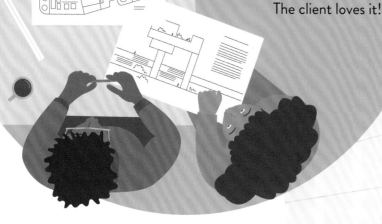

2

After the meeting, I start on the apartment design. For this, I use a 3-D modeling program on the computer. I'll show this model to the client the next time we meet so they can really see how the building will look.

3

Next, I head to the job site of some apartments that are currently being built. I visit sites often so I can see how things progress. I talk to the site foreman who manages all the building work. Everything seems to be going smoothly.

4

The client meets me on-site. We're currently building the lobby of the apartment building, so I show her how it's going. I talk her through the next phases of construction and give her an update on the schedule we're working toward. Part of my job is looking after clients and making sure they follow the process— it can be a lot to understand!

5

Back in the office, I have a meeting with a landscape architect, who designs outdoor spaces. We're finalizing the designs for the gardens at the apartments we're currently building. The plans include lots of beautiful trees. I think it looks great!

ALL KINDS OF ARCHITECTS

There are a number of different specializations within architecture. Restoration architects specialize in renovating and conserving old buildings. There are also lighting architects who design the lighting systems, both natural and electric, within buildings.

6

I finish the day and head home. Now, it's time for my hobby: building a model of a house I hope to have myself one day!

MY JOB: BEST AND WORST PARTS

BEST: Walking inside a building that was once one of my drawings is an amazing feeling.

WORST: It can be tricky working with clients who keep changing their mind about what they want.

ART TEACHER

I'm an art teacher at a high school where I teach a wide range of skills, including ceramics, drawing, and painting. To become an art teacher, I majored in fine art in college, then got my teaching credential. Working with my students and seeing their amazing creations is my favorite part of the job—it's fulfilling to see their work and know that I taught them the skills!

Art teachers also work in elementary schools, community colleges, and universities. Some teachers might also lead private classes for adults, hold summer camps for kids, and more.

1

Before my teaching day begins, I check the art supplies I have and what needs to be restocked. I'm running low on watercolor and oil paints, small brushes, and sketch paper, so I make a note to order more.

2

I start my first class. We're making clay pots. Working with wet clay is very messy, so everyone wears an apron. I show the students how to mold pots out of clay with their hands. To keep it soft and easy to shape, I add water to the clay as I work. I finish my demonstration, and then it's their turn.

MY JOB: BEST AND WORST PARTS

BEST: I love watching my students grow and develop their talents.

WORST: I don't get as much time with the students as I'd like—I wish we could make art together all day!

3

The students get to work, and everyone does a great job! At the end of class, I put each pot aside. In about a week, once the pots are totally dry, I will fire (bake) them in a kiln.

4

I have a free period next, so I do some lesson planning. I work on a class for my pottery students where they will learn how to paint and glaze their pots. I need to make sure that the students learn lots of different techniques and keep building up their skills.

5

My afternoon class is working on self-portraits with charcoal. I've asked them to bring in a photograph, and class begins with a demonstration. I work from a photograph to sketch myself in charcoal. Charcoal can be smudged to create lighter and darker tones, which is important when drawing faces because faces aren't one color! After the demonstration, the students grab their materials and get started.

7

The school day ends, but it's not time to go home yet. I run an after-school art club once a week. Here, the kids are free to use the art supplies to create whatever they'd like. I share some of my favorite portraits with the students to inspire them. Some love them, and some don't, but that's okay—that's what art is all about!

6

I walk around the room and talk with students about their work. One girl is disappointed—she feels like she's messed up her portrait. I can see that the nose she's drawn is too big in proportion to the eyes. I explain where she's gone wrong and encourage her to start over. Art is all about learning—I want my students to understand that mistakes are part of the process!

POLICE SKETCH ARTIST

I use eyewitness accounts and evidence from crime scenes to draw sketches for the police department. Simple sketches of a face are an important way of identifying people who may have committed a crime. I have a bachelor's degree in fine art and took classes in anatomy and composite drawing, which taught me how to draw different facial structures.

1

I start my morning at the scene of a burglary. I talk to a neighbor who caught sight of the suspect. I ask her to describe, in her own words, the person she saw.

2

She tells me about the person's facial features, but understandably it's a little hard for her to remember every detail. I have a portfolio of faces that I carry with me that shows all kinds of different facial features and structures. I ask her to pick the faces that are closest to the person she saw.

In addition to police sketch artists, there are also artists who work in courtrooms, drawing the people involved in trials.

3

I sit with her and begin to sketch the suspect in pencil, using the facial types she's chosen. As I work, I ask her more questions about the face she saw. It takes a long time to get a sketch right, so we break for lunch.

4

In the afternoon, I finish up the sketch. I ask the neighbor what she thinks—she asks me for a few adjustments, including hairier eyebrows. Once she's happy with it, she signs the back of it. The portrait will be used on TV and in newspapers to help identify the suspect.

5

When I finish work, I head to an evening class I've been taking. I'm learning to use an online program to create a digital facial reconstruction. I love learning new skills that will help me in my job!

MY JOB: BEST AND WORST PARTS

BEST: My art skills provide a service to my community, and that feels really good.

WORST: Sometimes it can be sad talking to people who are the victims of crime.

16

ART CRIME INVESTIGATOR

I work for a government criminal investigation agency, investigating art forgeries and stolen art. (Art forgery is the crime of creating and selling fake or copied artwork.) It's the perfect job for someone with an inquisitive mind who likes asking questions. You've got to really care and know about art. It takes dedication and hard work to solve crime!

I earned a degree in criminal justice before joining the agency. I've always had an interest in art, so after working here for a number of years, I joined a team that specializes in solving art crimes. I trained on the job, and learned about art history and the techniques used by forgers.

1

This morning, I'm meeting with a man who believes he might have bought a fake painting. He thought it was by a famous artist, and he spent a lot of money on it, so he's very worried!

2

I meet him at his home and take a look at the painting. It has been signed by the artist—but the spelling of the name is wrong! This seems like a silly mistake for a forger to make, but it does happen.

3

Next, I examine the provenance of the painting. The provenance is the history of an artwork, including documents that may accompany an artwork with information, such as its previous owners. There's a lot missing here. The provenance of real art is usually very detailed, so that's another telltale sign of forgery.

4

We need more evidence, so I take the painting to be examined by a forensic scientist. The scientist will use a microscope to check how old the paint is—if the provenance says the painting is older than the paint is, then it's a forgery. We should get the results in a few days.

5

I finish the day writing a report of the case so far, and planning my next steps. I'll need to make contact with the forgers without them knowing I'm an investigator. That's called going undercover—an exciting part of the job!

MY JOB: BEST AND WORST PARTS

BEST: It's satisfying to get all the answers I need to solve a case.

WORST: But, it's so frustrating when I can't!

CHILDREN'S BOOK ILLUSTRATOR

My job is the best! I draw and paint pictures for children's books. I come up with ideas for my own books, and I'm also hired to illustrate books that other people have written. There are different ways to become a children's book illustrator, but I earned a degree in illustration. I work from my studio—a room in my house!

1

I start the morning by emailing the designer at the publishing company that will print and sell my book. She's sent feedback on my pencil sketches, so now I can paint. I spend time finding references for the colors I'll use.

Some illustrators work on graphic novels—books in a comic-strip format that tell a story almost entirely through artwork.

2

The designer has asked me to draw a leafy background, so I add it to the design. Over the top of the pencil sketch, I use watercolors to paint the green background, and then the tiger. It looks great with the greenery—getting feedback from the designer really improves my work.

3

In the afternoon, I paint the next page, which shows the girl. She needs to look the same throughout the book—this is called continuity. It's fun bringing her to life. She looks like me when I was a kid!

4

When my work day ends, I clean the brushes so they're ready to use in the morning. I take a look at my storyboard—a plan of the pages I'm going to draw—and decide what I'll paint tomorrow. Once all the pages are ready, I'll scan them to my computer and send them to the publisher. I can't wait for children to read the book!

MY JOB: BEST AND WORST PARTS

BEST: It's so wonderful when I get letters and emails from my readers!

WORST: Working alone every day can sometimes be a bit lonely.

TECHNICAL ILLUSTRATOR

I create detailed drawings to help people understand information that explains how to use, build, or fix things. The company I work for makes electrical appliances, so my illustrations are used for instruction manuals, posters, and websites. I studied graphic design and illustration in college, and then did some apprenticeships when I graduated.

1

I start my day by drawing diagrams for a vacuum cleaner instruction manual. I have the written instructions and the vacuum cleaner, so I can draw it and its attachments exactly. My illustrations need to be realistic and clear so that people looking at them understand them easily. Using pencils, I sketch some drawings that I'll use as a plan.

2

Using the sketches, I then work up detailed illustrations on a computer program. As I draw, I think about which angles will best show how the vacuum cleaner works.

My illustrations give information, so I have to draw everything as accurately as possible. It's a job for someone with a good eye for detail.

3

In the afternoon, I do some reading about the smoothie maker that I'll be creating illustrations for next. I need to get to know the products really well in order to show other people how to use them!

4

I finish the day by meeting with my coworker from the sales department. The company is launching a new hair dryer soon, and I've been asked to create some diagrams for online sales material. I like this part of my job— when my illustrations help advertise the products.

MY JOB: BEST AND WORST PARTS

BEST: It feels good that my work helps people to understand complicated things.

WORST: There's no room for error— if I make a mistake, someone might struggle to use a product.

PHOTOGRAPHER

I've always enjoyed using cameras and taking pictures. While I was in high school, I worked at a photography studio, and then I majored in photography at art school. I was an assistant photographer for two years, and then I started my own photography business. I get to use my creativity every day and each photo shoot is unique, which is great for me—I never get bored with what I'm doing!

Photographers can specialize in different areas, such as wedding, newspaper, or food photography, or portraits. Along with being creative and good with people, a photographer needs to know lots of technical information.

1

I arrive at my studio and get ready for my first shoot. This morning I am taking pictures for a cat food ad. I set up the background, props, and lighting for the shoot. I look through my camera to check the shadows and colors, and I adjust the lighting.

2

My models—a boy and his cat— arrive. I shoot lots of pictures throughout the morning. I take a variety of shots, moving the models and my props and changing the lighting until I'm happy with the pictures I have. The shoot ends and the models head home— they did great!

3

A local tourism office has hired me to take some pictures of a river in my town. It's a local beauty spot, and they want to use the pictures in a new brochure. I grab my camera and spend a few hours there, taking pictures of the river from different angles until I get the perfect shot. Thankfully, the weather is beautiful today!

4

Back at my studio, I download the photos of the river from my camera onto my computer. Using photography software, I edit the photos; I crop the image to remove a person who was taking a walk by the river, and I make the colors look brighter. I need to pay attention to all the details to get the best picture. Once I'm happy, I email the pictures to the client.

5

For the rest of the afternoon, I shoot a still-life image—a collection of objects arranged in a specific way—that I'll submit to a photography competition. There's a cash prize for the winner. I'm hoping that my work will be good enough to get noticed by the judges.

6

I have another shoot tomorrow, so I prepare for it by checking my equipment, and making sure that the props are ready to use. I finish my day by calling the models to check that they will be at my studio by 10:00 a.m.

7

Then, it's a quick dash to the local community college where I've been invited to speak to a photography class. The students are waiting with their cameras, and I talk to them mostly about the art of composition—how to best arrange things for a photo. It's a really fun evening. I love talking about photography!

MY JOB: BEST AND WORST PARTS

BEST: There's such a great atmosphere on photo shoots. It's busy and exciting!

WORST: Equipment for my job is expensive—it's a disaster when something breaks.

INTERIOR DESIGNER

When I was little, I had a sketchbook filled with ideas for my dream bedroom. Then, I earned a degree in interior design, and now I work at a small company, helping people to make the insides of their homes functional and beautiful. I advise clients on how I think their home should be decorated, but they have the final say on the overall design. I work closely with my clients as well as furniture makers and painters.

2

Next, I check in with the electrician who has been installing new lighting in the house. He tells me that he's running late as there are some faulty wires that need to be replaced. I'll need to let the client know about the delay. In my work, meeting deadlines is crucial, but things don't always go according to plan.

I have to be super organized since there are lots of different things to keep track of at once. I also have to be good at talking and listening to people. Being creative and having a good imagination is just part of it!

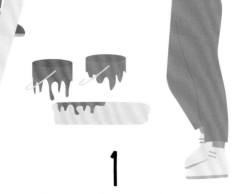

1

For my first job of the day, I check in on the progress at a client's home. I speak with the painter who is working on the living room walls. I chose warm orange and green colors for the decor to help make the space feel cozy. It's looking great! It's satisfying to see my ideas come to life.

3

A box of vases has arrived at the house. I check that there hasn't been any damage caused during delivery. Thankfully, they are in perfect condition! Once the house is ready for the furniture, the vases will be unboxed and set up along with the rest of the decor.

MY JOB: BEST AND WORST PARTS

BEST: I love using my creativity to make homes look beautiful.

WORST: Sometimes I don't agree with the client's wishes on interiors, but I have to follow orders—the customer is always right!

4

I head back to my office because I'm meeting some clients in the afternoon. I visited their home last week to get a feel for the space, and today I'll help them decide on a decorative style. They want a modern look for their home, so I've prepared some fabric swatches (samples), color schemes, sketches, and photos of furniture and lamps that might work.

5

I welcome the clients and take them through the design. The last time we met, they told me they enjoy cooking, so I've got lots of great ideas for their kitchen. I suggest some really bright red and yellow colors—and they are impressed! Getting to know my clients is one of my favorite parts of the job.

6

For my final task of the day, I finish some sketches and section plans (architectural drawings) for a bedroom design I'm working on for another client. I use my computer to draw the sketches, making sure that my measurements are correct.

7

My day ends and I head home to relax. Being comfortable is important to me, so when I designed my own home, I made it as cozy as possible. I think my cat loves it too!

GRAPHIC DESIGNER

I've always liked computers as well as drawing, so I decided to study for a degree in graphic design. Now, I'm a graphic designer at a design studio. I work with lots of different companies and clients to digitally design and create things such as websites, packaging, posters, brochures, branding, and logos.

1

For my first job of the day, I'm working on a poster for a dinosaur movie. The movie producers have hired my design studio, and they want it to look bold and exciting! I do some research on classic movie posters for inspiration.

2

I show my coworker my research and ask for her opinion. Working like this is really useful because often talking with others about ideas sparks new ideas! As we talk, I sketch on paper. We agree that the poster should feature the huge T. rex from the movie. It's going to look amazing! I'll do some more work on it a little later.

I work alongside other designers and the studio manager, who leads our team and helps us manage our work.

3

Next, I'm designing a new logo for a local gym. I've been given a brief (a set of instructions) by the gym owner. They've asked me to come up with something that will remind people of movement. I play around with different colors and shapes. I think a zigzag logo looks best, but I email the client a few options for her feedback.

4

Along with the studio manager, I meet a potential new client from a furniture store. The client explains that they want us to design their new brochure featuring their tables and chairs, and tells us the deadline we'll need to meet. The meeting goes well—I'll design a rough draft of the brochure the client wants, and I will work with them over the next few weeks to get it exactly right.

5

In the afternoon, I continue working on the poster from the morning. With the sketches I drew as a plan, I create the first design of the poster using a computer program. I show it to my colleague. She likes it, but she suggests that we make the dino—and his teeth—even bigger!

6

For my final job of the day, I am giving a presentation to a client from a national chain of stores. It's a big deal, so I'm nervous! But I take a deep breath, show my designs for their new website, and talk them through the color options. They like what I've done—phew! They'll take my designs away to choose their favorite and think about any changes they might want.

7

It's the end of my day, and I head home. Art is my hobby as well as my job, so I grab my sketchbook and get busy drawing!

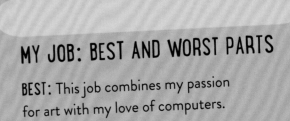

MY JOB: BEST AND WORST PARTS

BEST: This job combines my passion for art with my love of computers.

WORST: I sit in front of my computer for most of the day, so I don't move around much. That can make my back and shoulders ache!

ADVERTISING ART DIRECTOR

Have you ever wondered how ads are made? Well, my job is to dream them up! I started out as a graphic designer, and now I work in the creative department of an advertising agency. I design campaigns for products that people will buy in stores, and for newspapers, magazines, and TV. I love that I can be creative, but in this job, you need to learn to accept criticism—not everyone will like your ideas all the time!

To get my job, I studied graphic design in college. Along with coming up with ideas, my job involves choosing typefaces (the design of letters and words), arranging words and photographs, and instructing photographers and illustrators.

1

I start the day by checking in with my team of graphic designers (see page 24). I like this part of the day—it's great to see the progress everyone is making on different campaigns, and to take time to discuss any challenges or difficulties.

2

I spend time on a campaign for a new breakfast cereal. (A campaign is a series of ads, including posters, billboards, TV, magazines, and radio, for one thing.) The company has asked for an animal character for their campaign. I research other cereal campaigns, then draw some sample sketches of an aardvark character. I'll show these ideas to my coworkers for their feedback.

3

I spend the rest of the morning working on some sketches for a magazine ad for a new shampoo. A copywriter writes the words for the ad, and together, we come up with a snappy headline and an eye-catching layout (the placement of the images and words) that will appeal to readers. I decide that the shampoo bottle should be front and center, and I choose some on-trend pastel colors for the ad.

4

In the afternoon, I oversee a photo shoot for athletic apparel at a photographer's studio nearby. The ad we're shooting is my idea, so I need to oversee its production, and make sure that my plan is closely followed.

5

The photographer takes pictures of the models wearing the clothes. She follows the brief I've given, for the models to pose like they are playing sports. I just remind him that the brand's logo needs to be visible in the picture at all times. Seeing my plans come to life in this way puts a huge smile on my face!

6

I head back to the office. Next, I show the shampoo ad ideas to the creative director. (Creative directors have the final say on creative decisions within a company.) She thinks the colors should be bolder and the shampoo bottle should be even bigger in the ad. Once we've made these changes, I will pitch the ad to the shampoo company for their feedback. I hope they like it.

7

Next, I email an illustrator to see if he's available to work on an ad for a new restaurant. I spotted his work on social media—he draws pictures of vegetables that I love, and I think he'd be perfect! I send him details of the work—fingers crossed he's interested.

8

My day ends and I leave the office. I take the train home and pick up a magazine—and I see an ad in it that I created. It's amazing to think that what I hold in my hand, started out as an idea in my head!

MY JOB: BEST AND WORST PARTS

BEST: Creating attention-grabbing advertising is a challenge I love.

WORST: As the manager of a team, I have people who rely on me, and sometimes that can be stressful.

WALLPAPER DESIGNER

As a kid, I had lots of fun doodling designs and patterns. I studied fine art in college, and now I have a wonderful job as a designer at a wallpaper manufacturer. I've spent a lot of time developing my skills and my style, so it's really satisfying to see a whole room decorated with my work!

1

I begin my morning by showing the creative director a sketch for a design. Lots of factors inspire my designs, such as materials and colors that are trendy, or popular movies. I've read that there's a new TV show about robots, so I've created a cool design to coincide with its release that kids might want for their bedrooms! She loves it, and we decide to make it.

I need to study new trends and different styles of wallpaper made by other companies. I have to keep in mind what is popular, but I always want to create something fresh!

3

In the afternoon, a sample of a new nature-inspired wallpaper design comes in from the printer. I check how it looks and whether it needs any changes to the color or design. It all looks good, so I email them to say that they can go ahead and print the wallpaper.

2

I spend a few hours hand-drawing robots of different colors and sizes. I show the creative director, and her favorite is the silver robot, so I'll work more on that design.

4

I spend the rest of the afternoon at my desk, painting the robots I drew earlier. Tomorrow, I'll scan and upload them to my computer, where I'll use a program to edit the image.

MY JOB: BEST AND WORST PARTS

BEST: I can be really free and creative with my designs.

WORST: It's disappointing when a wallpaper design doesn't sell as well as I'd hoped.

TV SET DESIGNER

My job is to design the sets (backgrounds) of TV shows. It's creative and can sometimes feel glamorous! It's a popular career, so along with a degree in theater design, I needed lots of experience and internships to stand out from the crowd. You have to be able to work with others, manage under pressure, and explain your ideas clearly.

1
I'm on the set of a comedy show I've been working on. Before today, I read the show's script and then worked with the producer and director to design the set. I built a model to figure out the look and spacing of the set. With a model, I can clearly show my ideas.

2
I've designed the set to look like a living room because I want the viewers to get a cozy feeling when they watch the show. I speak with a stage technician who is finishing off a section of the wall. (Stage technicians construct, place, and move sets.) It's looking great!

In my job, no two days are the same. I often have to work out problems on the spot. I also have to do lots of research to get the right look for TV programs.

3
Next, I talk to a carpenter who is building the stairs. I ask her for an update on when she expects her part of the work to be done. She thinks it will take her about another week to finish. The set needs to be ready in two weeks, so it's tight—but I think we should be able to meet our deadline.

4
For my final job of the day, I check the budget against what's been spent on the set so far. I always have a certain amount of money that I can spend on a set, and I have to make sure I keep track of costs, including materials and labor.

5
When I finish work, I head to the theater to watch a new play. I get lots of inspiration from watching live performances. I'm always learning!

TICKET

SEAT: 72a ADMITS: 1

SEAT: 73a ADMITS: 1

MY JOB: BEST AND WORST PARTS

BEST: It still gives me a thrill to see my set designs when I turn on my TV.

WORST: I often have to work long hours to meet my deadlines.

GAME DESIGNER

It's my job to design the different levels (the stages that players work through) of a video game. I make sure the levels look great and are exciting and enjoyable to play. It takes a mix of artistic, planning, and computer skills. I studied interactive entertainment in college, then had internships and learned even more on the job.

1

Today, I'm designing a new level for a platform game—a game in which the player controls a character who can run and jump onto different platforms.

2

First, I roughly draw my idea for the level using pens and paper. I sketch out lots of things I think could be fun for the player. I add ladders to get from one area to the next, some floating bricks to jump over, and some water to fall into if they miss the jump!

My job involves analyzing and solving problems. I need to put myself in the position of the player and try to think about what might make them feel satisfied or frustrated.

3

Now that I've got my plan ready, I quickly input the rough design into a computer program. At this stage, it doesn't need to look good—I just need to be able to play it and test how it works. Games need lots of testing, even at this early stage, to work out any problems.

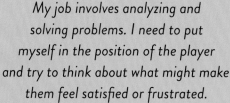

4

In the afternoon, I start testing the level. Right away, I find that jumping from the first platform onto the second is too hard, and it will be frustrating for the player. I'll need to change my design and place the platforms a little closer together.

MY JOB: BEST AND WORST PARTS

BEST: I get to play video games for my job. It's awesome!

WORST: Sometimes I have great ideas ... but can't make them work in the game!

5

I use the computer program to change the platforms, and I start testing again. I keep testing until the end of the day. I'll do even more testing tomorrow. Once the design is ready, it can be passed to a programmer who will code it into the game. That's the part I can't wait to see!

GAME ARTIST

Game artists create all the art seen in a video game, from backgrounds to characters and vehicles. I've been working as a game artist since I graduated from college with a degree in game art and design. The game I'm working on at the moment features animals racing go-karts—it'll be so fun!

Teamwork is vital in my job. I work closely with designers and other artists to bring our games to life!

1

Today, I'll be working on characters. I start by talking with the concept artist—who decides the art style of the game—and other game artists. The art throughout the game needs to have the same style. We all review the concept artist's sample sketches so we can follow them closely.

2

Next, I do research for some animal characters. I have the concept art, but I also need other references. I decide to work on a a giraffe character, and I find photographs of real giraffes online to study when I sketch.

3

After lunch, I sketch around 50 versions of the character. That sounds like a lot, but each one takes only about a minute. Tomorrow, I'll show them to the creative director. She'll choose her favorites and I'll draw them using a 3-D modeling program on my computer.

4

For the rest of the afternoon, I use the 3-D modeling program to work on some banners and flags that will be held by characters in the background.

5

I head home to eat dinner, go for a run ... and meet a friend to play video games! I like to think it counts as research.

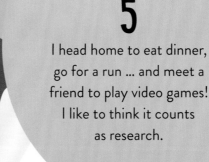

MY JOB: BEST AND WORST PARTS

BEST: I love working with other artists as part of a team.

WORST: I have really tight deadlines I have to work toward, and it can be a lot of pressure.

ART THERAPIST

As an art therapist, my job is to use art to help people manage their emotions and express themselves. It's very fulfilling. I earned a bachelor's degree in fine art, completed a master's degree in art therapy, and then became certified. I love helping people communicate through art.

Creating art can help people to feel less anxious, and more relaxed and confident. I work with people on their own and in groups.

1

My morning begins with preparing my studio. Some children are coming to me for a group session. I set out lots of different materials, such as paper, paints, crayons, and clay, for them to work with.

2

The children arrive and sit down. I tell them to create an image of a place that makes them happy. I ask them to first take a few moments to think about the task, and we sit together quietly. Then, they begin!

3

Once they're done, I meet with each child individually. Using the art that they have created, we talk about how they feel. One of the most important parts of my job is listening, so I let them do the talking.

MY JOB: BEST AND WORST PARTS

BEST: When a client feels better because of a session, that's something that will help them for a long time.

WORST: Some days are filled with paperwork and no creative sessions— I don't like those days as much!

4

The session ends and I say goodbye to the children. For the rest of the morning, I make notes about the session. I need to keep detailed records about each client's progress and think about what activities might be useful for our next session.

5

A doctor calls me about one of her patients who she thinks could be helped by art therapy. This is called a referral. I have some appointments free next week, so we agree on a time for the session. I'm looking forward to meeting the patient.

6

Next, a new client comes in and he's a bit nervous. I understand why he feels this way, but I explain that he doesn't need to know anything about art—it's not an art class and there's no right or wrong. I show him the different kinds of art materials we'll be working with.

7

I show him pictures of works of art and ask his thoughts on them. His answers could help me to understand his mood. I encourage him to make marks on paper based on some of the things we've looked at together. He seems to relax—I think he's enjoying himself!

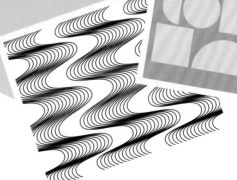

8

My working day ends, but I decide to stay a little longer and create some of my own art. I put on some music and make a collage using different materials. I find that expressing myself through art is good for me, too.

ART HISTORIAN

I work in a museum as an art historian. It's a fascinating job. Every day, I see amazing pieces of art. I investigate art, learn about it, write about it, and also teach other people about it! To get my job, I had to study a lot—I earned a bachelor's degree, a master's degree, and then a PhD in art history.

It's my job to find out as much as I can about the works of art that the museum owns or borrows. I also teach part-time at a university, so I spend a lot of my time talking to people.

1

For my first job of the day, I check an old painting. It's showing some signs of age, like cracks in the paint. I study it and write notes to show the conservator, a specialist who will inspect it further and work to restore the painting. I'm passionate about keeping the museum's art in the best condition possible—I want future generations to be able to enjoy the art like I can!

2

After I finish my notes, I start researching a sculpture that has been given to the museum. It's exciting to have it! I'm doing some research on the previous owners of the sculpture, so I read the provenance documents that came with it.

3

As part of my research on the sculpture, I call another museum that has a sculpture by the same artist in its collection. They invite me to visit soon to study their sculpture and its documents so that I can compare it to ours. I can't wait! Meeting other people who are as passionate about art as I am is such a great part of my job.

4

After lunch, I attend an acquisitions meeting—a discussion about the works of art that the curator and museum director expect to get this year. Some art will be bought, some will be donated, and some will be borrowed from other museums. We talk about when we can announce on our website that the art will be coming to the museum. These pieces should bring lots of new visitors!

5

Next, I head to the university to give a lecture. It's on European medieval art, and I have some fascinating images to show the students. This is one of my favorite subjects to teach—it shows that humans have always loved creating art.

6

My lecture begins. I tell the students about medieval tapestries— long, woven wall hangings that were either decorative or told a story through the art. When the lecture ends, I answer questions.

7

I'm about to finish for the day, so I check my email to see if there's anyone I need to reply to. The last email of the day is an invitation to speak at an art history conference. They want me to talk about some of the art we have at the museum. I'm delighted to accept!

MY JOB: BEST AND WORST PARTS

BEST: My job lets me look at amazing works of art all day. What could be better?

WORST: It's hard when borrowed artwork is returned to its owner— I wish we could keep it all!

ANTIQUES APPRAISER

As a kid, I found my grandma's collection of antiques—her old pieces of collectable art—fascinating. Today, I'm an appraiser. I run a business examining people's antiques and estimating their value (how much money they are worth). I have a bachelor's degree in art history and I worked in an antique store for a few years. In my work, I see some truly amazing things!

1

Today, a sculpture has been brought to me to be valued. It's a gorgeous Art Deco piece, a style of art created in the 1920s and 1930s. The owner of the sculpture leaves it with me, and we arrange for him to come back in a couple of days.

2

To value this piece, I first spend time checking its condition. It looks like it's in great shape, with no damage or scratches—that's good! The better condition it's in, the higher the price should be.

People want to have their artwork valued so that they can sell it or have it insured (financially protected in case it's lost or stolen). That's where I come in!

3

The sculpture has documents with information about it, including the name of the artist. I spend the afternoon searching sales records in an online database for artwork by the same artist. This will help me figure out how much this statue might sell for.

4

At the end of my day, I get a call from a client about a painting. She wants me to value it, so I agree to visit her tomorrow. The client bought it several years ago for a lot of money. The value of art usually increases as time passes, so she's hoping that it's worth even more money now. It might not be, but making a thorough assessment and telling the truth is all part of my job!

MY JOB: BEST AND WORST PARTS

BEST: I love seeing the smile on a client's face when I tell them that their antiques are worth a lot!

WORST: Making a mistake and realizing that an antique I've valued is actually worth a lot less than I'd thought.

5

I finish my day by heading to the opening of a new exhibition at a local gallery. I know a lot of artists in town, so I get lots of invitations to art events. I'm fascinated by antiques, but I love seeing new art, too!

ART
Exhibition

10:00 a.m.
—
7:00 p.m.

AUCTIONEER

An auction is a sale where people bid—offer to pay a price—for goods. Items here are sold to the highest bidder. I manage the auctions and sell pieces of art. To get my job, I earned a bachelor's degree in art history, trained at auctioneer's school, then worked at an auction house. Today is an auction day. I can't wait to get out there!

1

I start my day by checking the order of the items—or "lots"—being sold. Before today, I inspected the items being sold and read lots of information about them, since I'll need to tell the audience about the art.

2

Next, I review the estimated value of each item, so I know how much it should sell for. Each item also has a minimum price decided by the seller, so that's where the bidding needs to start.

Being an auctioneer is like putting on a performance, so you have to be able to talk in front of a large crowd. It was a bit scary when I stood up at my first auction, but now, I find it exciting!

3

Each auctioneer has their own chant or style of talking to keep bidders engaged. My style is chatty, and I talk at a fast pace. Before the auction starts, I make sure to drink lots of water, and I also do a few vocal warm-ups.

4

Time for the auction to begin! The first lot is a sculpture. I talk about its history and the artist who made it. I start the bidding at the agreed minimum price. People hold up paddles to show they want to bid. I announce each bid made so everyone can follow along. A high bid is made and no bids top it, so I strike my gavel (a small hammer) which means it's sold!

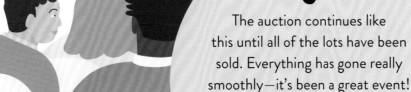

5

The auction continues like this until all of the lots have been sold. Everything has gone really smoothly—it's been a great event!

MY JOB: BEST AND WORST PARTS

BEST: Feeling the tension and excitement grow during a sale is like nothing else.

WORST: Trying to listen to all the bidders at the same time can be a lot to handle!

ARTIST-IN-RESIDENCE

I'm a painter, and this month, I'm working as the artist-in-residence at a natural history museum. This means I'm working at the museum for a period of time creating art inspired by my surroundings and the people who visit and work here. I've been working as an artist full-time for a number of years, and when I saw the opportunity, I applied and was accepted! My residency will last for a month.

Artists-in-residence work all over the world in organizations such as museums, hotels, offices, and schools, and each residency is different. It's very exciting work!

1

For my first job of the day, I'll be creating sketches of visitors. Observing and sketching the things around me is part of my artistic process— hopefully it will spark some ideas for paintings.

3

Next, I continue with a painting in one of the collection rooms that houses dinosaur bones. The museum director asked me to paint this, but I've also been given lots of freedom to do what I like. Visitors come to talk to me, so my painting is going slowly, but talking about my art here at the museum is a part of the job and I enjoy it.

2

As a group of visitors arrive, I tell them a little bit about myself and my residency. Then, I ask if I can draw them. They agree, so I take out my journal and sketch them studying the artifacts on display.

4

As part of my residency, I've been asked to write articles for the museum's website to document my experiences here. Over lunch, I write about what I've done today, and make notes on ideas for other articles.

5

I've been given special access to some of the museum's collections, which means that I can see artifacts that aren't on display. I spend time sketching and taking photos. It's making me feel really inspired! Seeing "behind the scenes" of the museum is one of my favorite things about this work—it's such a privilege.

6

Next up, I'm leading a session with a group of schoolchildren. I ask them to explore the museum and draw their favorite things. It's lots of fun! The children all want to draw something different, and I love helping them use their imaginations.

7

I end my day by meeting with the director of the museum. We chat about the work I've done so far. I tell her that I'd like to create a painting inspired by the artifacts I saw "behind the scenes." She loves the idea! I can't wait to get started.

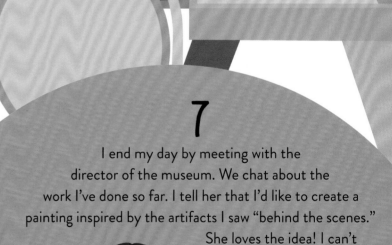

MY JOB: BEST AND WORST PARTS

BEST: It feels good that the art I create is a tool to inspire others.

WORST: It's a short-term role, so even though I feel like I could work here forever, I can't!

ART GALLERY OWNER

I run a small art gallery. Along with selling art to customers and managing a small staff, I'm responsible for choosing the art that is sold here. My bachelor's degree in arts management and master's degree in art history gave me the tools to do my job. In this job, you have to be good at talking to people, as well as having an eye for art that people will want to buy.

An art museum displays art for people to admire and enjoy, but in a commercial gallery, art can be bought by customers. Artists are "represented"—this means that both the artist and the gallery make money from any art sold.

1

Before I open, I listen to some music while I make sure that the gallery is ready for customers. The staff arrive at 8:45 a.m., then at 10:00 a.m., I unlock the doors and start the day.

2

It's quiet in the gallery this morning, so I spend some time looking through a portfolio (a set of work) I've been sent by a new artist. This is one way I find artists, but I also go to art colleges and exhibitions organized by the artists themselves. After looking at this portfolio, I decide that, although I like the work, it's too similar to other art I have at the moment, so I won't be representing them.

3

Next, I spend time writing a newsletter. I send this out to previous customers to let them know about new artworks for sale. I need to encourage people to buy from the gallery so that we make money—keeping in contact with regular customers is a good way to do this. I write about some really beautiful portraits of famous people by a talented new artist and send the letter out.

4

In the afternoon, the gallery gets busier. A customer is looking for a painting for his new home. I ask him about his likes and dislikes, so I can get a feel for the right piece of art. In this job, listening skills are important—I have to listen to my customers to help them find what they need. He tells me that he likes bright colors, so I show him a painting that might be to his taste. He loves it and decides to buy it.

5

The gallery closes at 5:00 p.m., but my day's not over. Tonight, I'm hosting a special evening exhibition to celebrate the work of an artist I represent. I hold these exhibitions every month to showcase new work. I've invited a number of previous customers who I think might be interested in buying new pieces. The event starts in an hour, so my team and I begin getting the gallery ready for guests. We set out some chairs and rearrange the gallery so the artist's work is the main display.

6

The artist arrives ahead of the event. She's a graffiti artist—she uses spray paints to make art. She's prepared a talk about her artistic process. I show her where she'll be speaking and chat with her. It's almost 6:00 p.m., and we open our doors. I spend time greeting guests and meeting new people. Being friendly is an important part of this job—I want to give people a good experience so that they come back again.

7

It's great to see the gallery full of people! I introduce the artist. She tells us about how she uses bright, neon colors to create her fun-looking art. It's fascinating to listen to. Once she finishes, I talk with as many people as I can about the art on sale and make recommendations to people who want to buy paintings.

8

The event ends and the gallery empties out. The customers were so inspired by the artist's talk that all of her paintings have been sold. I finish my day by recording the sales. It's been an amazing success!

MY JOB: BEST AND WORST PARTS

BEST: I'm always on the go, which is great because I love being busy!

WORST: Sometimes we have quiet weeks when we don't sell very much. That can be a bit worrying.

INDUSTRIAL DESIGNER

I work for a company that makes bicycles and their accessories. I use my art skills to visualize and design the products. Industrial design is about working out how products look, work, and fit together. To get my job, I earned a degree in industrial design.

1

Today, I'm designing a basket for a bicycle I've been working on for the last few months. I start out by making some sketches.

2

Next, I copy the sketches onto a computer program called CAD (computer-aided design). With this, I can create a virtual 3-D model and can see different angles and perspectives. The CAD also keeps track of the dimensions and measurements, which will be given to the factory when the product is made.

Besides bikes, industrial designers create all kinds of products and appliances, from hair dryers and food processors to smartphones and cars.

3

I spend the afternoon tweaking the design. I try out different ideas, such as sleek, rounded corners, until I'm happy with it. An important part of my job is making sure that my creations are visually appealing to people who might buy them.

4

I finish by making a model of the pieces that will fix the basket to the bike. Tomorrow, I'll show it to other designers on my team, and I'll make some changes depending on their feedback. The next stage is for a prototype (a test model) of the bike and the basket to be made. I can't wait to see it!

MY JOB: BEST AND WORST PARTS

BEST: I get to use really cool, cutting-edge computer software.

WORST: Sometimes, we get to the prototype stage and realize we have to change the design. Then, it's back to the drawing board.

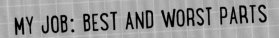

TEXTILE DESIGNER

I work for a children's clothing company. My job is to create the designs that will be printed on the fabric. It's a career for someone with lots of creativity! I studied textile design in college and learned all about how to work with different kinds of materials. Then I got an internship at this clothing company and worked my way up to a full-time job.

1

Today, I'm designing a pattern for a T-shirt. I spend the first part of my morning researching the latest trends in kidswear. I look up what other companies are working on and check social media sites to see what styles, colors, and themes are trending. From my research, I think a shirt inspired by things found at the beach will be popular with customers and look really fun.

2

Over the next couple of hours, I create a mood board—a collage made up of fabrics, colors, and patterns to inspire me as I draw. I include swatches of blues, yellows, and greens since these colors make me think of the beach. I also pin up some pictures of shells, pebbles, and sand.

Along with clothing, textile designers also design fabric for home furnishings, such as sofas, cushions, carpets, and curtains.

3

I start sketching with the mood board by my side. I play around with a few different motifs (small drawings that will be repeated to form a larger pattern). I draw lots of things that remind me of the beach, including a seashell, a boat, a fish, and an octopus.

4

In the afternoon I run my designs by my colleagues. They all love the octopus motif, so I draw it in more detail. The T-shirt will be made from cotton, but my mood board has gotten me thinking of the rough texture of sand. I make a note to speak to the manufacturer about how we can add texture to the pattern when it's printed on the cotton.

5

Finally, I scan and upload my drawing to the computer. I play around with it and turn the single motif into a repeating pattern. Tomorrow, I'll show my design to the marketing and sales teams for feedback. Fingers crossed they love it!

MY JOB: BEST AND WORST PARTS

BEST: I love the creative process and gathering things that inspire me!

WORST: Sometimes the textures and fabrics I want to use are too expensive.

YOUR PERFECT JOB MATCH

With so many different jobs to think about, it can be tricky to choose the right one. This guide will help you identify your skills, interests, and personal qualities to see which job might suit you.

Police sketch artist

Art therapist

Photographer

Art teacher

Great communicator

If you're good at talking to people, consider these careers.

Advertising art director

Art crime investigator

Antiques appraiser

Precise

Architect

These jobs suit people who are good with the details.

WHAT ARE YOUR SKILLS?

Game designer

Technical illustrator

Graphic designer

Good with technology

Industrial designer

These jobs are perfect for those who like working with computers.

Interior designer

Organized

Art gallery owner

Art museum curator

Some jobs need people who are good at making plans.

Textile designer

Furniture maker

Practical

Wallpaper designer

TV set designer

These careers are ideal for those who like working with their hands.

Top Panel

Antiques appraiser

Art historian

Advertising art director

Auctioneer

Curious

Confident

Art crime investigator

Art teacher

If you like asking questions, these jobs may be for you.

WHAT QUALITIES DO YOU HAVE?

Consider these jobs if you like taking the lead.

Game designer

Artist

Industrial designer

Independent

Patient

These jobs are great if you like working on your own.

Children's book illustrator

Architect

Taking time to get things right is important in these jobs.

Bottom Panel

Art teacher

Art therapist

Artist

Furniture maker

Helping others

Wallpaper designer

Police sketch artist

If you enjoy helping people, you'll like these jobs.

WHAT ARE YOUR INTERESTS AND GOALS?

Making things

Textile designer

Photographer

Meeting new people

For people who like making new friends, these jobs are perfect.

Artist-in-residence

If you're good at turning your ideas into reality, these are the jobs for you.

Art museum curator

Art gallery owner

45

THERE'S MORE ...

You've read about a lot of art careers in this book, but there are many more to choose from. Read on to discover seven more exciting jobs for people who love art.

MAKEUP ARTIST

A makeup artist uses their artistic skills with makeup to enhance a person's features. They might work in a hair and beauty salon, a department store, or for TV and movie studios. For someone who loves art, fashion, and working with other people, this would be the perfect job.

CAKE DECORATOR

Cake decorators use their baking skills to bake cakes, and then their artistic flair to decorate them in all kinds of amazing ways. They need excellent attention to detail and great hand-eye coordination. This job is perfect for someone who is a whizz in the kitchen!

CARTOONIST

Cartoons are exaggerated drawings that tell a story, either in a single image or in multiple images. A cartoonist might be published in newspapers or online, and their cartoons can be funny or serious. This is a job for someone with great drawing skills, a unique style, and the ability to create their own stories.

JEWELER

Jewelers create and repair jewelry, including rings, bracelets, and earrings. Along with designing pieces, jewelers use tools to weld (join) and engrave (carve) pieces. They often work with precious metals and gemstones. It's a practical job for someone who likes putting their ideas into action.

FASHION STYLIST

A fashion stylist advises people on what to wear. A stylist should be aware of the latest fashion trends, as well as different clothes, textures, and color palettes. They might work for a company on photo shoots, or work for individual clients. For someone who loves clothes and fashion, this is the perfect job.

LANDSCAPE ARCHITECT

While architects design the structure of buildings, landscape architects design outdoor spaces, such as gardens, parks, and golf courses. For this job, you need excellent drawing and planning skills, a knowledge of building and engineering, as well as training in horticulture (the science of growing plants).

BOOK COVER DESIGNER

A book cover attracts people to pick up and read a book. Covers need to look stylish, and give customers an idea of what the book is about. A cover designer works with book editors and illustrators to come up with amazing designs—so it's a job for someone who likes collaborating with others. If you've got great computer skills, this could be the ideal career for you.

First American Edition 2021
Kane Miller, A Division of EDC Publishing

Copyright © 2021 Quarto Publishing plc

Published by arrangement with Ivy Kids, an imprint of The Quarto Group.
All rights reserved. No part of this book may be reproduced, transmitted
or stored in an information retrieval system in any form or by any means, graphic,
electronic or mechanical, including photocopying, taping and recording,
without prior written permission from the publisher.

For information contact:
Kane Miller, A Division of EDC Publishing
PO Box 470663
Tulsa, OK 74147-0663
www.kanemiller.com
www.edcpub.com
www.usbornebooksandmore.com

Library of Congress Control Number: 2020936349

Manufactured in Guangdong, China CC 102020

ISBN: 978-1-68464-168-0

1 2 3 4 5 6 7 8 9 10